HANDA'S HEN

EILEEN BROWNE

WALKER BOOKS
AND SUBSIDIARIES
LONDON • BOSTON • SYDNEY

Handa's grandma had one black hen.
Her name was Mondi – and every morning
Handa gave Mondi her breakfast.

One day, Mondi didn't come for her food.
"Grandma!" called Handa. "Can you see Mondi?"
"No," said Grandma. "But I can see your friend."
"Akeyo!" said Handa. "Help me find Mondi."

Handa and Akeyo hunted round the hen house.

"Look! Two fluttery butterflies," said Akeyo.

"But where's Mondi?" said Handa.

They peered under a grain store.
"Shh! Three stripy mice," said Akeyo.
"But where's Mondi?" said Handa.

They peeped behind some clay pots.
"I can see four little lizards," said Akeyo.
"But where's Mondi?" said Handa.

They searched round some flowering trees.

"Five beautiful sunbirds," said Akeyo.

"But where's Mondi?" said Handa.

They looked in the long, waving grass.
"Six jumpy crickets!" said Akeyo. "Let's catch them."
"I want to find Mondi," said Handa.

They went all the way down to the water hole.

"Baby bullfrogs," said Akeyo. "There are seven!"

"But where's … oh look! Footprints!" said Handa.
They followed the footprints and found...

"Only spoonbills," said Handa. "Seven … no, eight.
But where, oh where is Mondi?"

"I hope she hasn't been swallowed by a spoonbill –
or eaten by a lion," said Akeyo.

Feeling sad, they went back towards Grandma's.
"Nine shiny starlings – over there!" said Akeyo.

"Listen," said Handa. ^{cheep}_{cheep} "What's that?"

^{cheep}_{cheep} ^{cheep}_{cheep} ^{cheep}_{cheep} ^{cheep}_{cheep}

"It's coming from under that bush.

Shall we peep?"

Handa, Akeyo, Mondi and ten chicks

hurried and scurried and skipped back to Grandma's ...

where they all had a very late breakfast.

hen

mice

lizards

butterflies

sunbirds

crickets

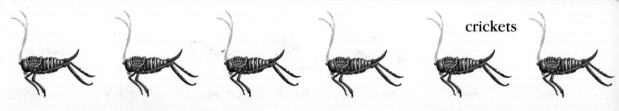